What Lives in the
Dirt?

WORMS

CRABTREE
PUBLISHING COMPANY
WWW.CRABTREEBOOKS.COM

CRABTREE
PUBLISHING COMPANY
WWW.CRABTREEBOOKS.COM

Published in Canada
Crabtree Publishing
616 Welland Avenue
St. Catharines, ON
L2M 5V6

Published in the United States
Crabtree Publishing
PMB 59051
350 Fifth Ave, 59th Floor
New York, NY 10118

Published in 2020 by Crabtree Publishing Company

First published in Great Britain in 2019 by Wayland
Copyright © Hodder and Stoughton, 2019

Printed in the U.S.A./122019/CG20191101

Author: Susie Williams

Editorial director: Kathy Middleton

Editors: Victoria Brooker, Ellen Rodger

Designer: Lisa Peacock

Illustrator: Hannah Tolson

Production coordinator and prepress: Margaret Salter

Print coordinator: Katherine Berti

Library and Archives Canada Cataloguing in Publication

Title: Worms / by Susie Williams and [illustrated by] Hannah Tolson.
Names: Williams, Susie, author. | Tolson, Hannah, illustrator.
Description: Series statement: What lives in the dirt? |
  Previously published: London: Wayland, 2019. | Includes index.
Identifiers: Canadiana (print) 20190195126 |
  Canadiana (ebook) 20190195142 |
  ISBN 9780778773894 (hardcover) |
  ISBN 9780778773986 (softcover) |
  ISBN 9781427125040 (HTML)
Subjects: LCSH: Worms—Juvenile literature.
Classification: LCC QL386.6 .W55 2020 | DDC j592/.3—dc23

Library of Congress Cataloging-in-Publication Data

Names: Williams, Susie, author. | Tolson, Hannah, illustrator.
Title: Worms / by Susie Williams and Hannah Tolson.
Description: New York : Crabtree Publishing Company, 2020. |
  Series: What lives in the dirt? | Includes index.
Identifiers: LCCN 2019043491 (print) | LCCN 2019043492 (ebook) |
  ISBN 9780778773894 (hardcover) |
  ISBN 9780778773986 (paperback) |
  ISBN 9781427125040 (ebook)
Subjects: LCSH: Worms--Juvenile literature.
Classification: LCC QL386.6 .W535 2020 (print) |
  LCC QL386.6 (ebook) | DDC 592/.3--dc23
LC record available at https://lccn.loc.gov/2019043491
LC ebook record available at https://lccn.loc.gov/2019043492

WORMS

CRABTREE
PUBLISHING COMPANY
WWW.CRABTREEBOOKS.COM

By Susie Williams
and Hannah Tolson

Worms live in damp, muddy soil.
They wriggle through the soil searching
for dead plants and animals to eat.

Worms are very common.

In one field, there could be
more than one million worms.

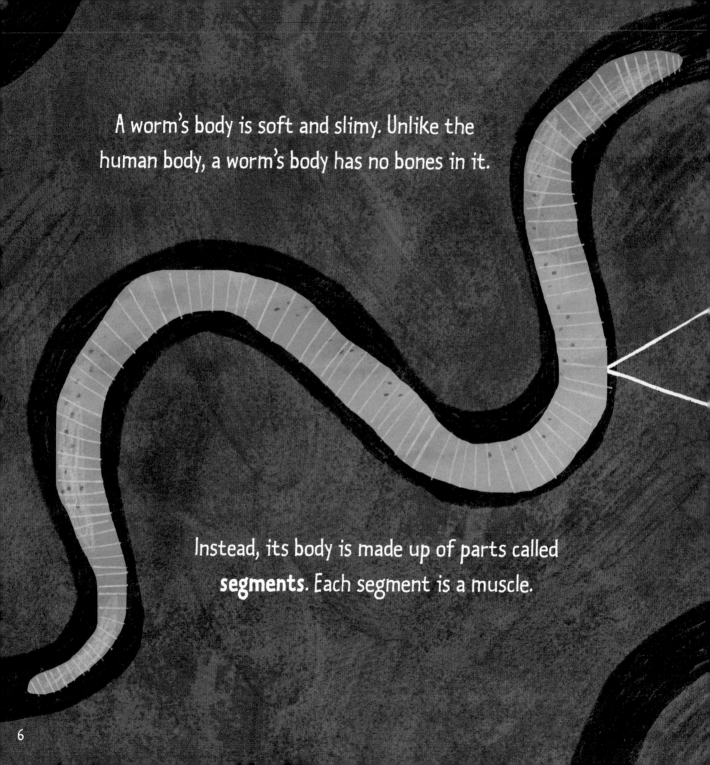

A worm's body is soft and slimy. Unlike the human body, a worm's body has no bones in it.

Instead, its body is made up of parts called **segments**. Each segment is a muscle.

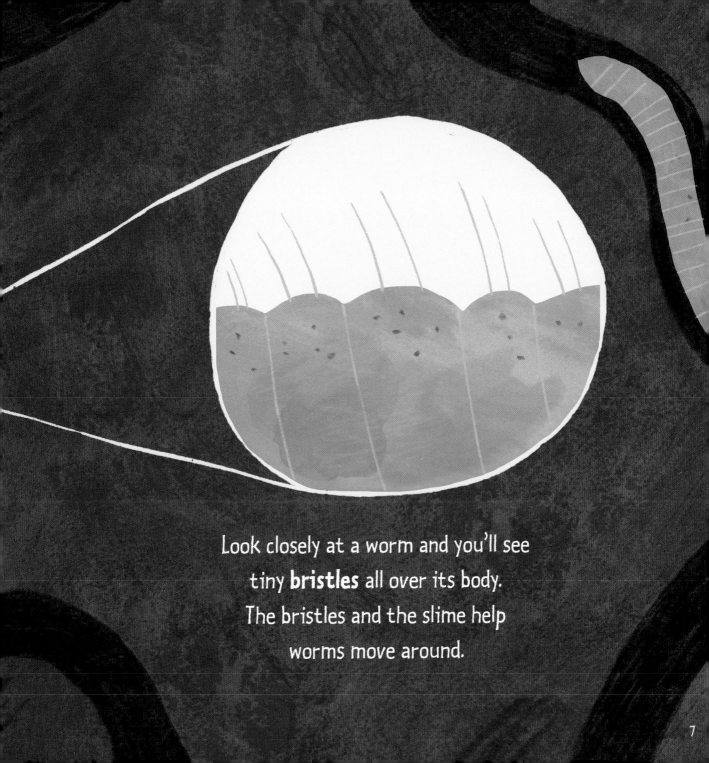

Look closely at a worm and you'll see
tiny **bristles** all over its body.
The bristles and the slime help
worms move around.

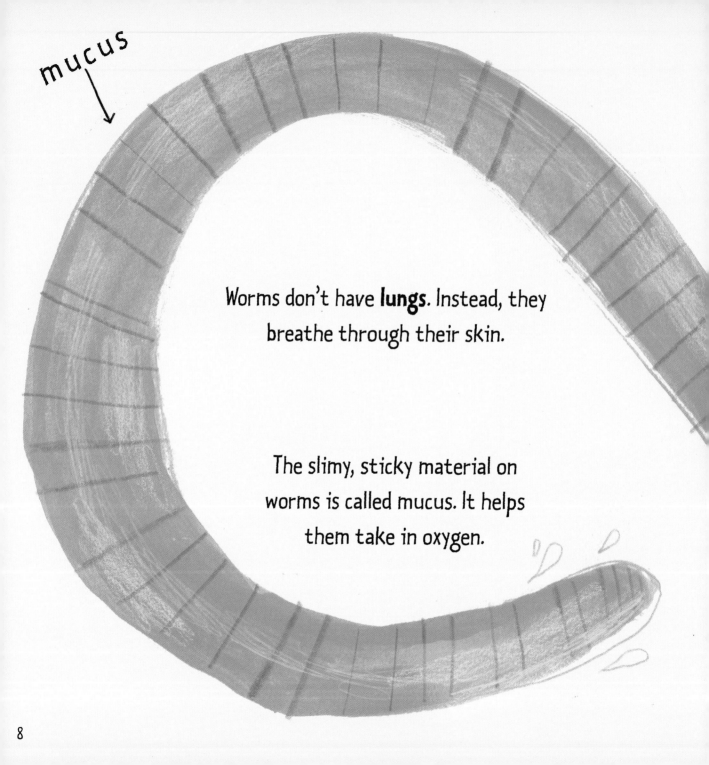

mucus

Worms don't have **lungs**. Instead, they breathe through their skin.

The slimy, sticky material on worms is called mucus. It helps them take in oxygen.

Humans have one **heart**,
but worms have five!
Worm hearts are tiny,
but very important.

hearts

As the hearts squeeze, they send
blood throughout the body.

Worms don't have eyes,
but they can sense
when it is light.

Bright sunlight isn't good for worms.
It dries out the moist mucus on their skin.
They need the mucus to help them breathe
and move around.

If a worm is in warm sunshine
for more than one hour,
it will die.

When a worm senses light,
it quickly wriggles deep
into the dark soil.

11

Watch for worms when it's raining.
They come to the surface then when
the sun isn't shining, and the soil
is moist and easy to move through.

But birds like rain too. That's because
they know worms will appear, and
birds love to eat worms.

Rats, badgers, and toads
eat worms too.

13

Worms only eat dead things.
A worm's favorite food is rotting leaves.

They'll also eat small
dead animals.

Worms have no teeth. They have strong muscles in their mouth that help break down the food.

Worms can be found in **compost** heaps too.
Compost heaps are mountains
of rotting food and leaves.

It's easy to make
a compost heap.

apple
cores

egg
shells

If you pile up leaves
and old vegetable
peelings, worms will
soon move in.

leaves

banana
peels

potato
peelings

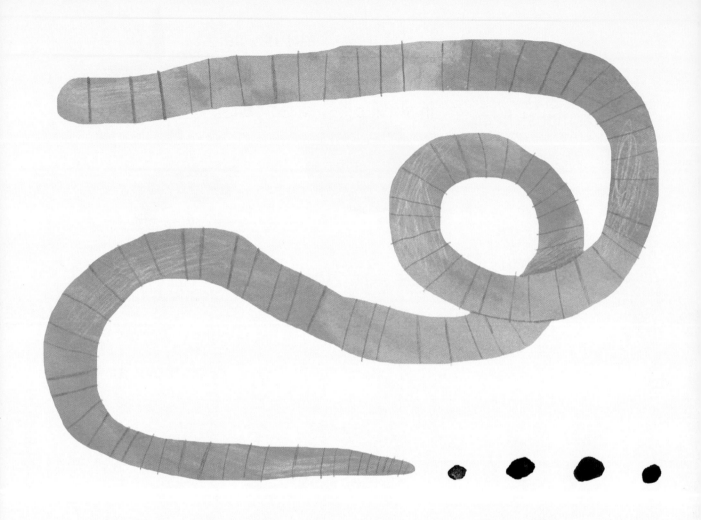

Worms poop as they move.
The poop is full of **nutrients**, which
makes the soil great for garden plants.

Their poop looks like small **pellets**.
Some earthworms' poop can be seen
in small piles, called casts.

Worms push the poop up out of the tunnels
they make in the soil.

19

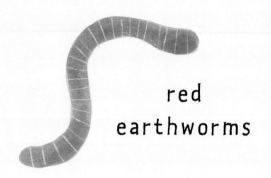

red
earthworms

blue
worm

There are thousands of
different types of worms.

European
nightcrawler

Some are so small that
you need a microscope
to see them.

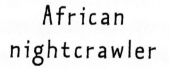

African
nightcrawler

red wiggler

The longest worm
is the African giant
earthworm.

It is 21 feet (6.7 m) long.

That's about 100 times
bigger than a garden
earthworm!

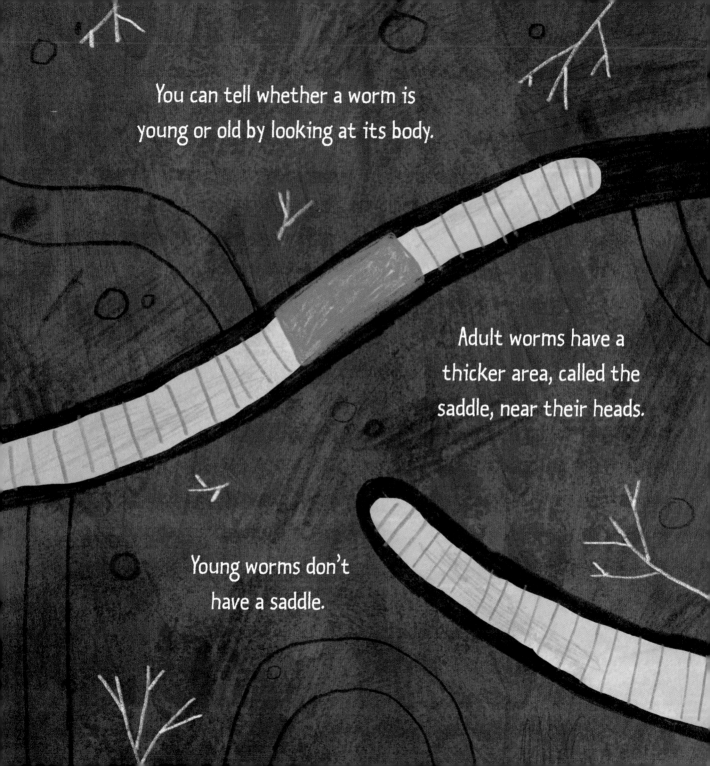

You can tell whether a worm is
young or old by looking at its body.

Adult worms have a
thicker area, called the
saddle, near their heads.

Young worms don't
have a saddle.

Worms can live for about six years.

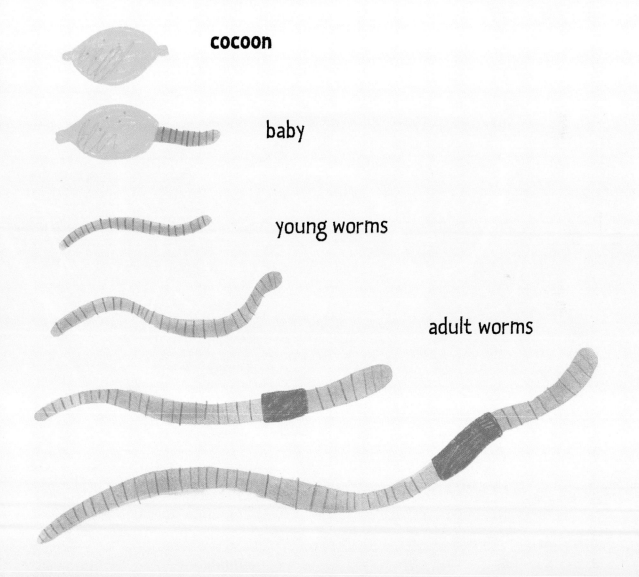

cocoon

baby

young worms

adult worms

Gardeners love worms.
When worms move through soil,
they leave little pathways.

The pathways let water and air into
the soil, helping roots grow.

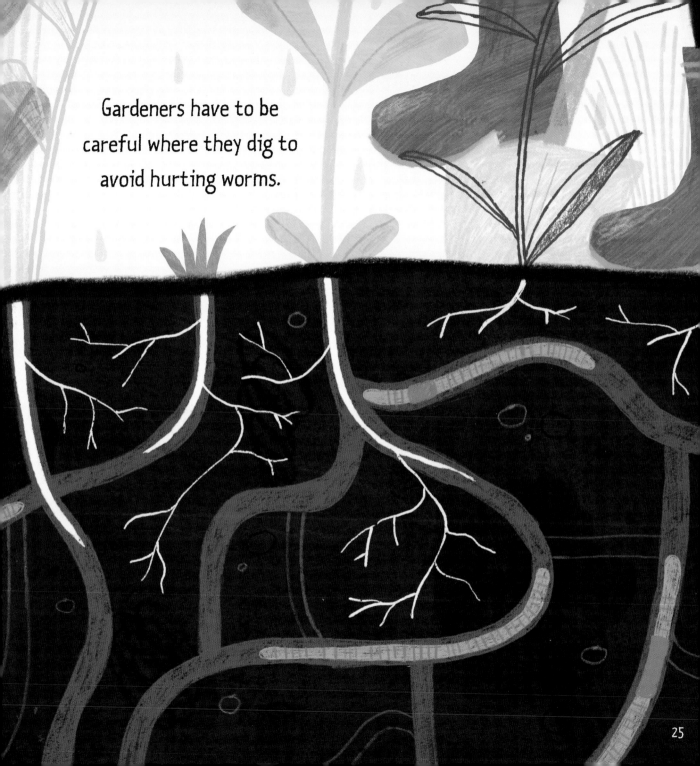

Gardeners have to be careful where they dig to avoid hurting worms.

25

Worms are amazing creatures. They get rid
of dead leaves and animals on the ground.

Their poop makes soil full of goodness
so that plants grow tall and strong.

Worms should be respected. So next time you see a worm, look at its amazing, wriggly body and slimy skin.

As you watch it disappear, think about how worms are helping to make your garden beautiful!

Make a wormery

A wormery is a kind of house to watch worms at work. It's where you can turn food waste into compost.

You will need:
- a large, clean glass jar
- jar lid with small holes in the top
- moist soil
- sand
- earthworms
- old leaves
- vegetable peelings, tea leaves, overripe fruit
- some black paper
- a cool, dark cupboard

1. Cover a table with newspaper. Put a layer of sand at the bottom of the jar, about 1/2 inch (1 cm) deep.

2. Add a thick layer of soil, then another thin layer of sand, then another thick layer of soil. Make sure to leave about a 2-inch (5 cm) space at the top of the jar.

3. Find some worms! Put the worms in the jar, then add some old leaves, vegetable peelings, tea leaves, and overripe fruit.

4. Put the lid on and tape black paper around the jar. The lid must have holes in it to let in air. Put the jar in a cool—but not too cold—dark cupboard.

5. Leave the jar for a couple of weeks. Check regularly to ensure the contents of the jar are moist—not too wet and definitely not too dry. Worms need dampness to be able to breathe.

28

After a couple of weeks, look at the jar. You should notice the vegetable peelings and leaves have nearly disappeared. Then put the worms back outside where you found them.

More wonderful facts about worms

Worms can be found in all parts of the world, except Antarctica.

There are about 34,000 types of worms.

The famous scientist, Charles Darwin, spent 39 years of his life studying worms.

For their size, worms are about 1,000 times stronger than humans.

Worms can eat as much food as their body weighs every day.

Glossary

bristles – Short, stiff hairs on an animal

cocoon – A covering made by young insects to protect themselves while they change into an adult

compost – A mixture of decaying leaves and vegetables that is used to improve garden soil

heart – The body part that pumps blood through the body

lungs – One of two body parts in the chest that are used for breathing

nutrients – Substances living things need to grow

pellets – Small balls of something

segments – One of the parts into which something is, or can be, separated

Index